YOURS 'TIL NIAGARA FALLS

WRITTEN BY **BRENDA Z. GUIBERSON**

ILLUSTRATED BY **WILLIAM LOW**

GODWINBOOKS

Henry Holt and Company

New York

Henry Holt and Company, *Publishers since 1866*
Henry Holt® is a registered trademark of Macmillan Publishing Group, LLC
120 Broadway, New York, NY 10271 • mackids.com

Our books may be purchased in bulk for promotional, educational, or business use. Please contact your local bookseller or the Macmillan
Corporate and Premium Sales Department at (800) 221-7945 ext. 5442 or by email at MacmillanSpecialMarkets@macmillan.com.

Library of Congress Cataloging-in-Publication Data.
Names: Guiberson, Brenda Z., author. | Low, William, illustrator.
Title: Yours 'til Niagara Falls / written by Brenda Z. Guiberson ; illustrated by William Low.
Description: First edition. | New York : Godwin Books, 2022. | Includes bibliographical references. | Audience: Ages 4-8 | Audience: Grades 2-3
Summary: "A thrilling, fact-filled history of Niagara Falls, following its evolution from the age of dinosaurs to its future disintegration"--
Provided by publisher.
Identifiers: LCCN 2021050306 | ISBN 9781627790994 (hardcover)
Subjects: LCSH: Niagara Falls (N.Y. and Ont.)--Juvenile literature.
Classification: LCC F127.N8 G85 2022 | DDC 971.3/39--dc23/eng/20211013
LC record available at https://lccn.loc.gov/2021050306

First Edition, 2022 • Book design by Mike Burroughs
The illustrations for this book were created using mixed media: ink, crayon, Adobe Photoshop, and Adobe Illustrator.
Printed in China by RR Donnelley Asia Printing Solutions Ltd., Dongguan City, Guangdong Province

ISBN 978-1-62779-099-4 (hardcover)
10 9 8 7 6 5 4 3 2 1

To PJ, who loves splashing, sparkling,
flowing water in all its forms —B. G.

To Malcolm —W. L.

Millions of years ago

NAUTILOID

TRILOBITE

**Millions of years ago, I was not a waterfall.
This was a time when ocean covered the land.**

Trilobites scooted over sand. Crinoids waved flowery arms.
Nautiloids hunted with long tentacles. Over the ages, their debris
piled up with layers of minerals on the ocean floor. These layers
hardened into rocks like dolostone and shale.

18,000 years ago

18,000 years ago, I was not a waterfall.
This was the time of the most recent Ice Age.

All the water was frozen into gigantic ice sheets, some almost two miles thick. These massive glaciers cut through the land. They gouged out gullies and trenches. Woolly mammoths and saber-toothed cats wandered over the whiteness.

12,500 years ago, the ice melted. Water flooded into gullies and trenches. Glacier lakes overflowed into rivers.

One river gushed thirty-four miles from Lake Erie to Lake Ontario. Along the way, it plunged over a steep cliff of dolostone and shale.

Crash! Roar! Sploosh!

That was me, the waterfall! Carrying one-fifth of Earth's fresh water, I cascaded, rumbled, roared, and tumbled. Birds swirled through my misty rainbow while fish and eels squirmed below.

Humans with stone tools came, following the large mastodons and herds of reindeer. They were amazed by my thundering voice.

I became a waterfall with many stories. They told of Hinu, the Great Thunderer, in the cave behind my cascading water. They told of the mischief of a great water snake. Later, other settlers made up stories about the Maid of the Mist, a beautiful spirit that appears in my shimmering mist.

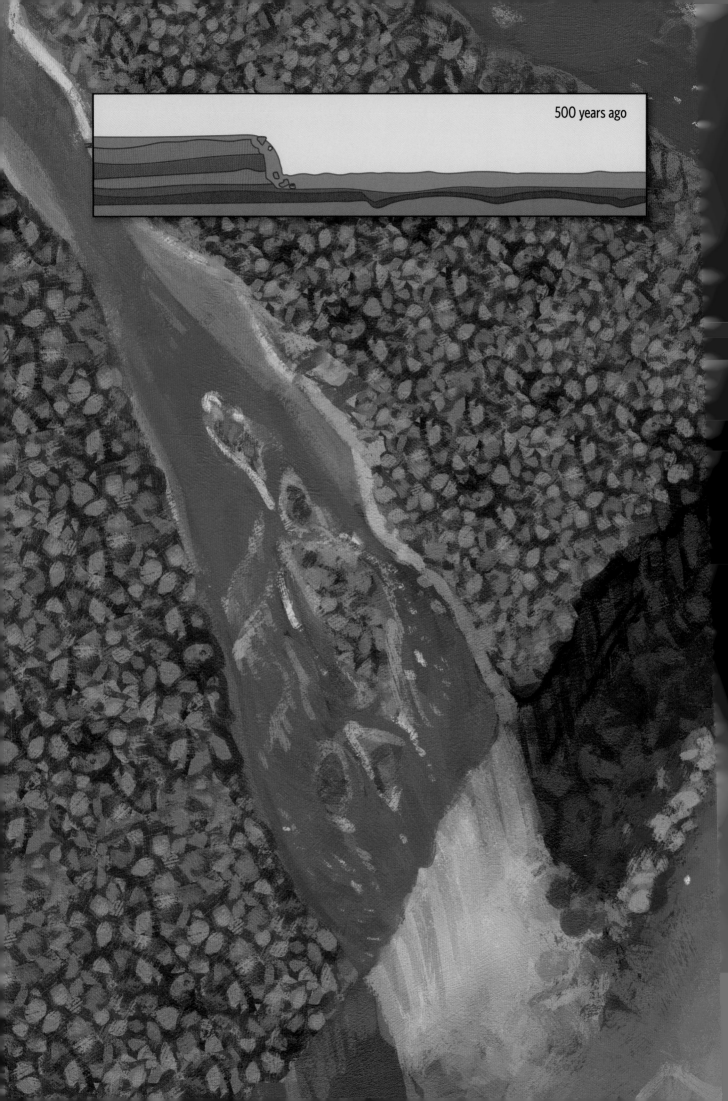

500 years ago

Year after year, my powerful flow cut into the layers of stone. As rock layers fractured and crumbled, I kept moving to new places in the river.

I was a waterfall reshaped by erosion. Five hundred years ago, I surged around an island thick with trees and ferns and split into two grand waterfalls. As always, some of my ancient glacier water evaporated to the sky. And sometimes water was added to my flow in the *plinkity-plunk* of raindrops.

In 1678, Father Louis Hennepin explored my wild and remote river. From far away, he heard my roar. Then he saw me.

He wrote about my "dreadful roaring and bellowing." He called me Niagara Falls, a waterfall that "has no equal." He even wrote that I fell 500 feet. That was an exaggeration. A better number might be 170 feet.

But around the world, people read these words.
I became a famous waterfall. Artists painted me.
Adventurers hiked in to get drenched in my mist and
hear my bellow.
ROOAAR!

In 1846, the *Maid of the Mist I* started sightseeing tours to Niagara Falls. By the 1850s, the railroads were bringing big crowds to see me. Forests and quiet riverbanks were replaced with tourists and hucksters.

CHARLES BLONDIN

CARNIVAL WHEEL

I became a waterfall of holidays and carnivals and a challenge for daredevils. In 1859, Charles Blondin crossed the Niagara River on a tightrope. He pranced and turned somersaults and carried a man on his back. The crowd gasped and cringed. Then Blondin danced across with a stove and stopped in the middle to cook some eggs. The Great Farini thought he could do better. He crossed with a washtub and pulled up a bucket of water. Then he washed his handkerchiefs and hung them to dry on his balancing pole.

THE GREAT FARINI

MAID OF THE MIST

In 1846, the *Maid of the Mist I* started sightseeing tours to Niagara Falls.

HARRIET TUBMAN

Some travelers arrived with enslaved people carrying luggage. For enslaved people seeking freedom, hotel employees whispered secret directions.

I was a waterfall on the Underground Railroad. In the moonlight, those hoping to escape to freedom crept down steep mossy stairs to my base on the American side. Then they snuck into a rowboat and were ferried out into the river. Drenched to the skin in my heavy mist, they crossed to the Canadian side to begin a new life. Others followed Harriet Tubman across the Suspension Bridge built just north of my thundering falls.

In 1875, the Niagara Falls Hydraulic Power and Manufacturing Company created power for factories in the Niagara Falls Mill District.

BRUSH ARC
STREET LIGHT

In 1881, the energy of my moving water was used to light up the streetlamps of Niagara Falls.

I became a waterfall of hydropower. Eventually more power plants were built and electricity was sent to Buffalo and beyond. As great volumes of the river were channeled into tunnels to create electricity, I had less water. This slowed the rate of erosion, but ledges of cracking rock continued to tumble around me.

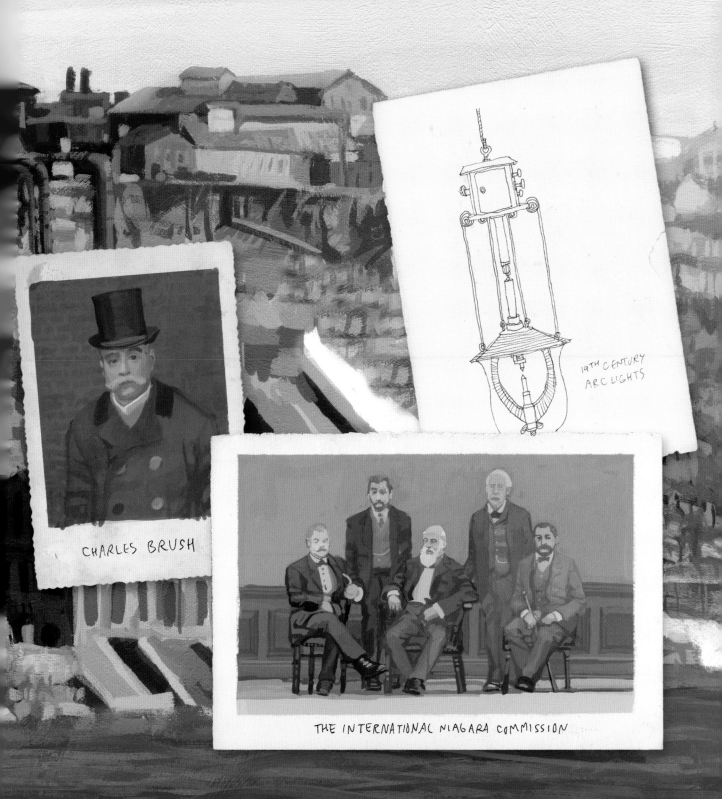

19TH CENTURY ARC LIGHTS

CHARLES BRUSH

THE INTERNATIONAL NIAGARA COMMISSION

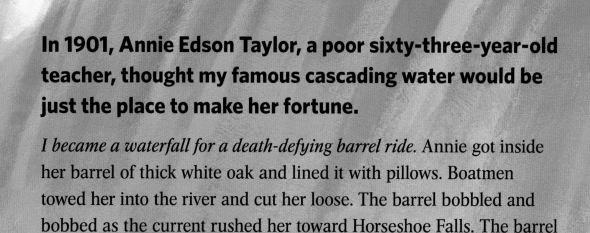

In 1901, Annie Edson Taylor, a poor sixty-three-year-old teacher, thought my famous cascading water would be just the place to make her fortune.

I became a waterfall for a death-defying barrel ride. Annie got inside her barrel of thick white oak and lined it with pillows. Boatmen towed her into the river and cut her loose. The barrel bobbled and bobbed as the current rushed her toward Horseshoe Falls. The barrel teetered at the edge. Then it plunged over my brink. They rescued her from the deep pool below. Later she sold five-cent postcards about the "Queen of the Mist."

Annie Edson Taylor

Trilobite fossil

EXPLORING THE DRY RIVERBED

BUILDING THE COFFERDAM

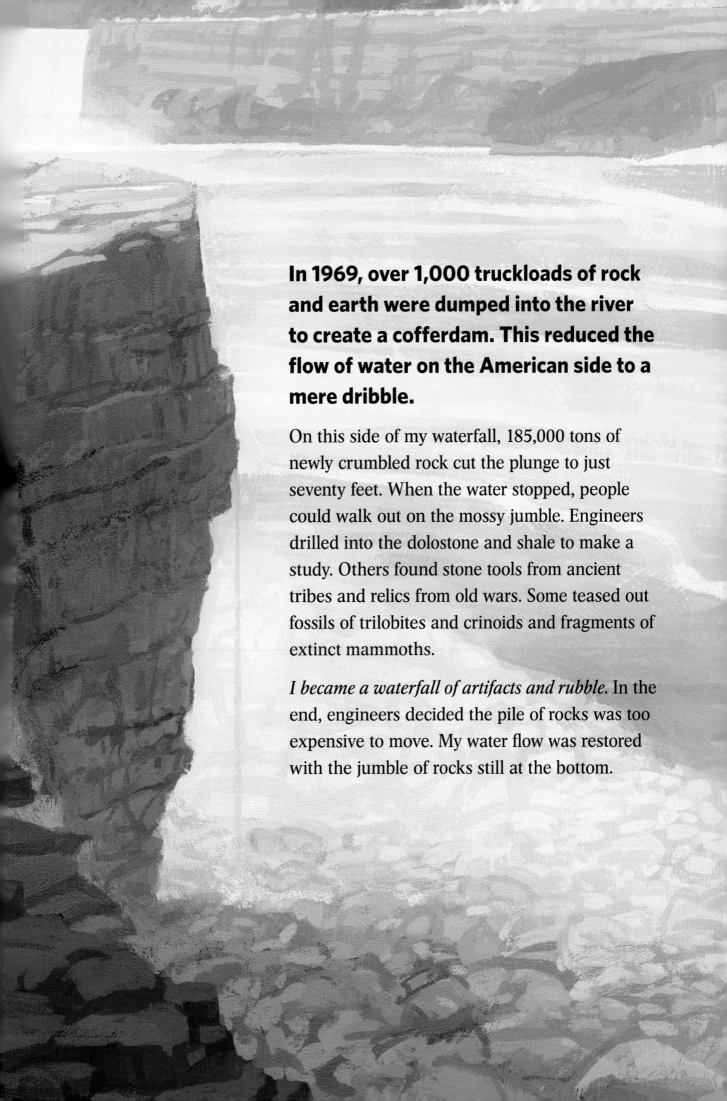

In 1969, over 1,000 truckloads of rock and earth were dumped into the river to create a cofferdam. This reduced the flow of water on the American side to a mere dribble.

On this side of my waterfall, 185,000 tons of newly crumbled rock cut the plunge to just seventy feet. When the water stopped, people could walk out on the mossy jumble. Engineers drilled into the dolostone and shale to make a study. Others found stone tools from ancient tribes and relics from old wars. Some teased out fossils of trilobites and crinoids and fragments of extinct mammoths.

I became a waterfall of artifacts and rubble. In the end, engineers decided the pile of rocks was too expensive to move. My water flow was restored with the jumble of rocks still at the bottom.

In icy winters, shifting winds can blow tons of ice over my falls. An icy bridge forms with many ice mountains, but still hundreds of thousands of gulls and ducks stop to eat and drink.

I am a survival waterfall as birds migrate to and from the boreal forest. Even in a frigid winter, when nearby rivers are completely frozen, some of my churning water is always available for the birds. In this bitter cold, I contain all the wondrous phases of water—solid, liquid, and gas.

In 1938, ice floes destroyed the Honeymoon Bridge.

Niagara Falls ice bridges were a popular tourist attraction.

Today, the *Maid of the Mist* ferries passengers ever so close to my deafening roar. *CRASH! SPLOOSH! RUMBLE!*

In the foam and mist, visitors sense the Stone Age maiden and Hinu, the Great Thunderer. They gulp the fresh air of enslaved people seeking freedom. They tremble with the rumble that creates electricity. They tingle with the challenge that calls to daredevils. *I am the waterfall that drenches them with mysteries of change across time.*

The power of my water is endless and erosion continues. Over many thousands of years, I will slowly move to new spots in the river.

Eventually I will reach Lake Ontario and wear down the last great layers of dolostone and shale. *I will be a waterfall no more.* Until then visitors can take a picture, touch the mist, or send a postcard. **"Yours 'til Niagara Falls"**

YOURS 'TIL
NIAGARA
FALLS
GUIBERSON · LOW

Bibliography

Allen, Nancy Kelly. *Barreling Over Niagara Falls.* Gretna, LA: Pelican, 2013.

Bauer, Marion Dave. *Niagara Falls.* New York: Aladdin, 2006.

Berton, Pierre. *Niagara: A History of the Falls.* New York: Kodansha International, 1997.

Bial, Raymond. *The Underground Railroad.* Boston: Houghton Mifflin, 1995.

Fisher, Leonard Everett. *Niagara Falls: Nature's Wonder.* New York: Holiday House, 1996.

Granfield, Linda. *All About Niagara Falls: Fascinating Facts, Dramatic Discoveries.* New York: Morrow Junior Books, 1988.

Strand, Ginger. *Inventing Niagara: Beauty, Power, and Lies.* New York: Simon & Schuster, 2008.

Van Allsburg, Chris. *Queen of the Falls.* Boston: Houghton Mifflin Harcourt, 2010.

Vanderwilt, Dirk. *Niagara Falls.* New York: Channel Lake, Inc. 2010.

Woods, Michael, and Mary B. Woods. *Seven Natural Wonders of North America.* Minneapolis, MN: Twenty-First Century Books, 2009.

Yates, Raymond. *The Niagara Story: Pictorial Guide to Niagara Falls.* Buffalo, NY: Henry Stewart, 1959.

Website Connections

niagarafallsundergroundrailroad.org/

niagarafallslive.com/Niagara_Falls_Interactive_Map.htm

audubon.org/important-bird-areas/niagara-river-corridor

niagaraparks.com/visit-niagara-parks/nature-gardens/

niagarafallsinfo.com/niagara-falls-history/niagara-falls-geology/niagara-geological-areas/
fossils-discovered-in-niagara/

niagarafrontier.com/origins.html#c

niagarafrontier.com/devil_frame.html

editors.eol.org/eoearth/wiki/Niagara_Falls

cnet.com/news/a-quadcopters-eye-view-of-niagara-falls/

Thanks to Laura Godwin, Rachel Murray, Sharismar Rodriguez,
Mike Burroughs, Gene Vosough, Alexei Esikoff, and Allene Cassagnol.

YOURS 'TIL
NIAGARA FALLS
GUIBERSON · LOW